CONCERNING SPIRITUAL GIFTS

Dean W. Nadasdy and
Thomas J. Doyle

Discipleship Series

CONCORDIA PUBLISHING HOUSE · SAINT LOUIS

Copyright © 1994, 2012 by Concordia Publishing House
3558 S. Jefferson Ave.
St. Louis, MO 63118-3968
1-800-325-3040 • www.cph.org

Study Guide written by Dean W. Nadasdy

Leader Guide written by Thomas J. Doyle

Editorial assistants: Megan Murphy and Ashley Bayless

Unless otherwise noted, Scripture quotations are from the ESV Bible® (The Holy Bible, English Standard Version®), copyright © 2001 by Crossway Bibles, a publishing ministry of Good News Publishers. Used by permission. All rights reserved.

Quotations from *The Lutheran Church and the Charismatic Movement*, a report by the Commission on Theology and Church Relations (CTCR) of The Lutheran Church—Missouri Synod, are copyright © 1977 Concordia Publishing House. All rights reserved.

This publication may be available in braille, in large print, or on cassette tape for the visually impaired. Please allow 8 to 12 weeks for delivery. Write to Lutheran Blind Mission, 7550 Watson Rd., St. Louis, MO 63119-4409; call toll-free 1-888-215-2455; or visit the Web site: www.blindmission.org.

Manufactured in the United States of America

1 2 3 4 5 6 7 8 9 10   20 19 18 17 16 15 14 13 12 11

Contents

ABOUT THE DISCIPLESHIP SERIES

If you abide in My word, you are truly My disciples, and you will know the truth, and the truth will set you free.

Jesus, in John 8:31–32

This course is one of several adult Bible studies in the Discipleship Series. The series was not designed to be a how-to course on specific work in the Church. It's not a manual for training evangelists or stewardship callers. It's not a practical handbook that can teach you church administration.

Rather, the purpose of this series is to help Christians dig into Scripture to explore some of the primary teachings of Christ Jesus. That's how disciples are made—by the power of His Word.

Therefore, this series is for people who, led by Christ, want to be His disciples. Some might be newly baptized or confirmed members of the Church who want to study further what they began learning in the pastor's membership classes. Others might be longtime Christians who want to review basic Christian teachings. Still others might be "seekers"—people who are puzzled by certain biblical teachings and want to find answers for their heartfelt questions.

The authors of these courses were selected because they, too, are Scripture seekers. Whether pastors or laypeople, they are avid students of God's Word, and they write with a desire to help guide fellow pilgrims in their search for truth. You'll find these courses easy to read and sympathetic to the seeking Christian.

This course has six 60-minute sessions, making it ideal for either a Sunday morning or midweek class.

INTRODUCTION

ABOUT THIS COURSE

This is a course about spiritual gifts—the special gifts given to particular Christians for the sake of specific ministries in the Church.

The first two sessions survey the receivers and the Giver—the context for the gifts. Sessions 3 and 4 examine the gifts. Session 5 provides an opportunity for participants to discover their own spiritual gift(s). Session 6 explores the fruit of the Spirit and how the fruit helps us use the gifts effectively.

Because of the extraordinary qualities of some of the spiritual gifts listed in the New Testament, many Christians shy away from the topic of spiritual gifts. They may be afraid of the topic or unsure of what to do with the biblical material about spiritual gifts. Worse, some people write off these passages as outdated and irrelevant to the Church today.

This course takes seriously what the Bible says about the gifts of the Spirit. The focus of the course is on you, the individual Christian looking for your niche in the Church, and on the congregation, the God-ordained gathering of believers around Word and Sacrament.

SESSION 1

THE GIFTED

THIS SESSION'S FOCUS

"You know, you're really a gifted person!"

How do you respond when someone compliments your gifts? If you're like many people, you smile, blush with embarrassment, and humbly glance downward, saying, "Me? Oh, not really." Why do we respond that way? Perhaps we're genuinely humble. Maybe we just can't see ourselves as gifted, or maybe we haven't yet discovered what gifts we have.

In this session, we learn that the Lord says, "You know, you're really a gifted person." The Early Church of the New Testament heard that good word from the Lord and celebrated it. They lived as if no people in history had been so blessed as they. Joy and thanksgiving abound in the New Testament, built on the realization of giftedness.

Times change. Christians today may need a little coaxing before they will believe how gifted they are. So this is where we begin our study of spiritual gifts, asserting that we are, indeed, gifted and ready for celebration.

OBJECTIVES

By the power of the Holy Spirit working through God's Word, the participants will

- recognize the need for gifts of the Spirit in the Church today;
- approach the study of spiritual gifts with a mood of gratitude and confidence;
- discover the joy and thanksgiving present in the New Testament Church as Christians recognized their giftedness; and
- celebrate God's gifts to His Church.

MEDITATION

As you know, I'm not usually one to complain.

Lately, though, let's just say that my mood needs some improvement.

It concerns Your church, Lord—our church.

Something is missing, but I can't put my finger on it. Something's just not right.

Why must we coax and twist arms for volunteers?

Why can't we do more?

Why do the same people do so much of the work?

And why do I hear so much about that *other* church, where everything good seems to be happening?

Lord, I'm not asking for full pews or new buildings.

I'm asking for a mood swing.

Long ago, Lord, people often said, "These men have turned the world upside down!"

That's how struck they were by the Church's fervor and Spirit.

Bring back that time to Your church, Lord.

Begin with me. Amen.

SESSION PRIMER

What are spiritual gifts? For this course, we will use the following definition:

Spiritual gifts are special gifts (1) given by the Holy Spirit; (2) given by the grace of God; (3) received by all members of the Church (that is, all members receive one or more gifts); (4) given to be used within the Church (but sometimes to touch people outside the Church); and (5) given to build up the Church.

Talk about the definition. Then respond to the following. Do you agree or disagree?

1. Most people in the Church today do not even know what their spiritual gifts are.

2. Ministry in the Church is primarily the task of pastors and teachers.

3. Every congregation has within its ranks the gifts necessary to carry on the Lord's work successfully.

BIBLICAL SEARCH AND STUDY

Search the Scriptures to discover the giftedness of Christ's Church.

1. The New Testament teems with expressions of thanksgiving and joy. Early Christians celebrated being Christ's Church. They knew God had gifted them. The basic verb for the action of giving (*didomi* in Greek) occurs in the New Testament over one hundred times with God, Jesus, or the Holy Spirit as its subject. Seven different nouns can be translated "gift" in the New Testament. The Church saw itself as the gifted people of God.

Read 2 Corinthians 8:9. According to Paul, to what do Christians owe their giftedness? Paul strikes a paradox here. What is it?

2. Read 1 Corinthians 1:4–7. For what is Paul grateful? What is the result of God's blessing?

Now examine Romans 12:6a; Ephesians 4:7–8; and 1 Peter 4:10. What do passages like these tell you about the grace of God? What does God's grace do for the Church?

3. The Early Church received grace upon grace from God. Joy and thanksgiving were fitting, natural responses. Still, some Christians missed how gifted they were. Their mood soured, and then prodding and reminding were needed to move them to thanks and joy. Sound familiar? What attitudes or practices work against a celebrative mood in churches? What could cause an abundantly gifted congregation to grow stale and cold? (See, for example, Revelation 2:1–5.)

Paul often had to exhort his congregations to a celebration of their gifts. Read Colossians 3:15; 1 Thessalonians 5:16–22; and 1 Timothy 4:4–5. In each of these passages, what reason does Paul give for thanksgiving and joy? What do these imperative passages tell you about the Church then and the Church now?

4. The image of the Body of Christ helps lead to a richer understanding of the Church as God's gifted people. Read 1 Corinthians 12:12–27. In a chapter about spiritual gifts, Paul talks about body parts, functions, unity, and diversity. After you examine these verses, list some truisms (self-evident truths) concerning the Church and its gifts.

5. Read 1 Peter 2:4–10. Peter creates a montage of the Church. What pictures comprise his montage, especially in verses 5 and 9? What does God ask of every Christian in Romans 12:1? Tell about times when you have seen this happen in your congregation.

What This Means for Us

Read the following letter.

Dear Pastor,

With this letter I resign from all my offices and duties in our congregation. You personally, Pastor, have done nothing to bring this about. I continue to love and respect you.

Specifically, I no longer wish to serve as Sunday School superintendent, congregation secretary, fellowship committee member, visitation committee member, and guild treasurer.

Pastor, I guess I'm just tired—bummed out, maybe. I don't feel I'm doing a good job. It seems as though I do nothing except go to meetings. I'm sure another person can bring more to these positions than I can. I'm concerned, too, about how much time I spend away from my family.

I'm asking for some time and some distance to rest and get renewed. I'll continue to worship and attend Bible class regularly. I may join the choir. Maybe someday I'll be ready for more active church work again. Right now, I need to step aside. I hope you understand.

In Christ,
Linda

1. What, in your opinion, is behind Linda's resignation? How does Linda's letter reflect characteristics of many Christian congregations

today? Why do you think she chose to resign from everything? Is Linda justified in her decision? What does Linda need most right now?

2. Consider yourself a present-day Peter or Paul writing to your congregation in the imperative (commanding) mood. What motivation would you present for the future life of your church, especially concerning gifts, thanksgiving, and joy?

3. A pastor once commented, "In the typical American Christian congregation today, 30 percent of the members do 25 percent of the work; the pastor does 25 percent; and 50 percent of the church's work never gets done." What do you think? Is the pastor correct?

4. Start to think about your gifts. Though we haven't yet looked directly at the lists of gifts in the New Testament, the Body of Christ metaphor provides some interesting aspects of giftedness in the Church. From the list below, choose three body parts and their functions that you think best apply to you and your gifts.

- Heart (shows love and compassion; is at the center of things)
- Eyes (sees opportunities and challenges; watchful)
- Ears (listens well)
- Kidney (helps cleanse and purify the Church)
- Feet (carries good news; a mover)
- Hands (makes things happen; builds)

- Head (learns easily; motivates; innovates)
- Neck (takes risks; sticks neck out)
- Arms (embraces; joins; reconciles)
- Mouth (speaks well and articulately)

What parts of the Body of Christ are represented in your group? Did you discover a diversity? Did anyone's choices surprise you?

GLEANINGS

What have you gleaned from the Scriptures today? Jot down a few notes on what you've learned, especially regarding the following: the Church's moods; the relationship between grace and gifts; the priesthood of all believers; your role in the Church.

THE GIVER

THIS SESSION'S FOCUS

The teacher of an adult Bible class began a new class with these words: "Let me introduce you to the Holy Spirit."

Some people in the class had been active Christians all their lives. They had been in church and in Bible classes for years. They had been baptized and confirmed. They had heard the invocation of the Trinity spoken thousands of times. They had sung their glorias to Father, Son, and Holy Spirit. Now their teacher presumed to suggest that he would introduce them to the Holy Spirit. Who did he think he was anyway?

However, the Holy Spirit does rank a poor third place for many Christians today. As a spirit, He may seem vague, distant, or elusive. Introductions are in order. Meeting the Holy Spirit is a little bit like meeting a person who has had a far-reaching impact on your life but has managed to stay nearly anonymous in the process.

In our last session, we found the Church to be a gifted group, God's own people who serve Him well. In this session, we will get to know the Giver of our gifts. Your leader might well open your class by saying, "Let me introduce you to the Holy Spirit."

OBJECTIVES

By the power of the Holy Spirit working through God's Word, the participants will

- survey the ministry of the Holy Spirit as revealed in the Scriptures;
- learn more about the Holy Spirit's work; and
- grow in confidence in the Holy Spirit as giver of gifts to the Church.

MEDITATION

Lord Christ,

It's about Your church again.

Not far from here is a church everybody's talking about.

Things are really happening over there, Lord.

I mean *really* happening.

Why, some of the young people from our church visit there and rave about it.

That church must be doing something right.

They say it's a Spirit-filled church.

Some strange things go on over there too, Lord.

I'm not sure I'm at all comfortable with their style.

Is that what a Spirit-filled church looks like?

Is it?

There are times, Lord, when my faith swells within me, and I feel as if I'm standing on the edge of heaven itself!

Is *that* being "Spirit filled," Lord?

Is it?

I guess I have a long way to go in understanding what Your Spirit is like, what He does, and how He would have me worship and live and love.

But I am willing to learn, Lord. I am. Please teach me. Amen.

SESSION PRIMER

Read aloud this quotation from Martin H. Franzmann. Then talk about it, using the questions provided.

> Still the Holy Spirit comes where and when it pleases God to send Him to proclaim the wonderful works of God. How will we respond? Will we stop short at amazement and perplexity, shaking our heads at some of His stranger (and lesser) manifestations? Will we even stoop to mockery at those manifestations of the Spirit which strike us as bizarre, so that we may ignore the rest of them and proceed to the usual order of business?

Or shall we find grace to go the way Jesus went under the impulsion of the Spirit—the way into the wilderness to meet and overcome the Tempter, the way into the Scripture and obedience to the Father's voice heard in the Scriptures, the way into self-consuming ministry and so into that life over which death has no more authority? Shall we find grace to go the way which the first church went in obedience to the Spirit?   (From Martin H. Franzmann, *Alive with the Spirit* [Concordia Publishing House, 1973], p. 8.)

According to Franzmann, how does the Spirit come? Where does the Spirit lead? Which of Franzmann's questions, in your opinion, presents the Church with the most timely challenge?

BIBLICAL SEARCH AND STUDY

1. The passages that follow create what might be called a "Spiritscape," a panoramic view of the Spirit's nature and work. Select one or more of the following verses. Then summarize what each reference says about the Holy Spirit.

Responses should focus on the Spirit's nature and work, that is, on what the Spirit is like and what the Spirit does. Be especially alert to the verbs describing the Spirit's actions and to the impact of the Spirit on people's behavior. You might wish to jot down key verbs and descriptive words as a summary of your search and study.

Genesis 1:1–2; Judges 15:9–17; 1 Samuel 16:11–13; Psalm 139:7–10; Isaiah 42:1–7; 63:10–14; Joel 2:28–32; Mark 1:8; Luke 4:14–21; John 3:5–6; 16:12–13; 20:21–23; Acts 2:1–4; Romans 5:5; 8:2, 5, 9, 11, 13–17, 26–27; 1 Corinthians 2:6–13; 3:16–17; 12:1–4, 7, 12–14; Galatians 4:6–7; 5:16–25; Ephesians 3:14–19; 4:1–4, 25–32; Philippians 3:3; Titus 3:4–7; 2 Peter 1:20–21.

2. Use the information from the Spiritscape to answer the following:
a. Who does the Holy Spirit have?

b. What are the Spirit's gifts meant to do?

c. How can we be sure that the Spirit is near, close to the heart of the Church?

d. What do all who have the gifts of the Spirit have in common? In what way(s) can those gifted by the Spirit be different?

3. As Luke by inspiration of the Holy Spirit (2 Peter 1:21; 1 Corinthians 2:13) recorded the Early Church's history, he saw the Holy Spirit behind every one of its growth spurts. Examine Acts 2:4; 4:8; 10:44–45; and 13:1–3. These passages from Acts affirm that the Holy Spirit empowered all these advances of the Early Church. Do you think the Church today has this confidence in the Spirit's direction of its future? Why or why not?

4. A person earnestly seeking the Giver and His gifts asks, "How can I be sure I have the Holy Spirit and His gifts?" How do you respond? For clues, see Luke 11:9–13; Romans 5:1–5; 10:17; 1 Corinthians 11:23–26; 12:13; and Titus 3:4–7.

What This Means for Us

1. If you were to begin a program of spiritual renewal, which of the following would be most feasible for you personally?

_____ a. Daily study of God's Word

_____ b. Regular, more focused prayer

_____ c. Support and nurture from Christian friends

_____ d. Memorization of important Scripture passages

_____ e. Scheduled "retreats" away from the daily routine

_____ f. Daily renewal of your Baptism

_____ g. More frequent participation in the Lord's Supper

_____ h. Involvement in the Church's mission

_____ i. Focus on discovering or developing your spiritual gifts

Are you willing to make a commitment to begin your program now? The Scriptures present few prerequisites for being filled with the Spirit and using one's spiritual gifts. The Scriptures encourage the use of the Means of Grace, prayer, and the fellowship of the Church as the context for spiritual renewal. Think about your life in the Spirit. Share with your group your plans for nurturing your spiritual life. What changes in routine will you need to make? When will you begin?

2. How do you most often view the Holy Spirit in your faith and prayer life? Choose one of these responses, and share it with a partner or your group.

_____ a. The One who calls, gathers, enlightens, and sanctifies the whole Christian Church on earth

_____ b. The half-known God, running a poor third in the Trinity

_____ c. A Friend I have not come to know

_____ d. The Giver of all my gifts, near me to bless me

_____ e. The person of the Trinity I wish we would talk about more

_____ f. The person of the Trinity who seems to belong to other denominations

We've learned that the Holy Spirit comes when and where He wills. We cannot program the Spirit's comings and goings. It can be exciting, however, to catalog His doings in the Church. On a separate sheet of paper, describe a time when the Holy Spirit richly blessed you. (It may or may not have been a time of great emotional exhilaration. The Spirit comes mightily at times and gently at other times.) Jot down the experience under headings such as "The Event" (perhaps your confirmation, a stirring moment in a worship service, or a time of testing in the hospital); "The People Who Surrounded Me" (if you were not alone); "The Feelings"; "The Means" (Scripture, Baptism, Lord's Supper); "The Outcome."

Share your event with your group. As you listen to others talk about their events, be alert to the rich variety of the Spirit's manifestations in His Church.

3. Talk about the Spirit's direction of your congregation's growth and ministry. Where especially have you seen the Spirit's blessings? What direction does He seem to have for you as a congregation in ministry? Tell about any surprises you've seen.

GLEANINGS

Summarize what you've learned in this session, especially in these areas: the Spirit's nature and work; your own need for spiritual renewal; and your congregation's life in the Spirit.

SESSION 3

THE GIFTS (PART I)

THIS SESSION'S FOCUS

We are gifted people, and the Holy Spirit is the Giver. The first two sessions have set the stage for the central focus of this course, spiritual gifts. In sessions 3 and 4, we will look closely at the lists of spiritual gifts in the New Testament, discovering just what spiritual gifts look like.

In a way, these sessions will look and sound like a gift-opening party. The mood is excitement for the Church—the joy and anticipation of peeling away the wrappings to discover the gracious gifts God has given to His people.

Recall the question we asked in session 1: What are spiritual gifts?

We answered this way: Spiritual gifts are special gifts

1. given by the Holy Spirit;

2. given by the grace of God;

3. received by all members of the Church (that is, all members receive one or more gifts);

4. given to be used within the Church (but sometimes to touch people outside the Church); and

5. given to build up the Church.

It may help us better understand what spiritual gifts *are* if we also look at what spiritual gifts *are not.*

1. Spiritual gifts are not the traits God gives to all Christians. For example, the faith of Ephesians 2:8 is given to all Christians, but not all receive the "spiritual gift" of faith (1 Corinthians 12:9). Every Christian is gifted with one or more spiritual gifts (1 Corinthians 12:11; Ephesians 4:7–11).

2. Spiritual gifts are not earned, but are received by God's grace (1 Corinthians 15:10a).

3. Spiritual gifts are not given so we can glorify ourselves, but for the building up and ministry of the Church (1 Corinthians 12:7; 14:12).

4. Spiritual gifts are not the fruit of the Spirit. (The fruit of the Spirit are listed in Galatians 5:22–23.)

Our focus is on spiritual gifts. In this session, we'll build a spiritual gift list on the basis of Scripture.

OBJECTIVES

By the power of the Holy Spirit working through God's Word, the participants will

- survey the gifts of the Spirit as they appear in the New Testament; and
- enhance their understanding of the role of spiritual gifts in the life of the Church.

MEDITATION

Lord, I looked around the church today, and I was overwhelmed. You know, Lord, we are quite a gifted bunch.

I'm sure I should have been listening to the sermon, but my eyes wandered over there to Grandma Lindsay, who keeps the prayer chain going. She's really something, Lord.

And young Tommy Schmidt, acolyte for the day. Everyone expects he'll be a pastor someday.

Everyone except Tommy Schmidt.

We'll see, Lord.

Then I glanced over at Mr. Garcia. Why, in all the church, I doubt if we could find a better teacher than him.

The kids actually love Sunday School!

And the pastor, looking tired but alive in Christ.

And the Washburns, who open their home to foster kids.

And Mrs. Brown, wearing her button again—"Thousands are hungry! Will we feed them?"

I looked at us, Lord, and I liked what I saw—the people You have blessed, who are now blessings to others.

Give us all eyes to see the gifts we have in the people who surround us in church. Amen.

SESSION PRIMER

Choose two people from your group to read the dialogue below. Imagine that speaker 2 holds a beautifully wrapped present with his or her name on it. Use the questions provided as a follow-up to the dialogue.

IT'S YOURS!

1: Well, look at you! What do you have there?

2: What does it look like?

1: Happy birthday!

2: It isn't my birthday.

1: Well then, whose birthday is it?

2: I don't know whose birthday it is.

1: May I look at it?

2: Sure, go ahead.

1: Why, this has your name on it.

2: I know. I saw that.

1: Then it's yours.

2: I told you, it isn't my birthday.

1: But the gift is yours. The tag says so.

2: I guess.

1: Then open it up, silly.

2: I'm not sure I should.

1: Why not? Of all the ungrateful—

2: I'm just not sure, okay?

1: Sure of what? It's yours! You're sure of that, aren't you?

2: Maybe. Who would want to give me a gift anyway?

1: I don't believe this. You get a gift, and you're not sure you want to unwrap it? What are you going to do, admire the wrapping?

2: I just wish I knew more about it. Where did the gift come from? What will be expected of me after I open it? Maybe I'll owe somebody something. Maybe I'll be disappointed.

1: Now *there's* a heroic approach to opening gifts. You must be great fun at Christmas.

2: Look, I didn't ask for your advice. As a matter of fact, I didn't even ask for this gift.

1: Well, it's yours anyway. But you're right; I won't talk about it any further. It's your gift and your decision. So what are you going to do? Hold it? Hide it? Look at it? Wonder about it? Throw it out? Waste it? What are you going to do?

1. In 1 Corinthians 12:1, Paul wrote, "Now concerning spiritual gifts, brothers, I do not want you to be uninformed." In verse 31, he wrote, "Earnestly desire the higher gifts." What causes some Christians to fail to discover their spiritual gifts?

2. Why do you think some congregations neglect an emphasis on the discovery and use of spiritual gifts?

3. What is the impact on the Church when people do not "open" their spiritual gifts?

BIBLICAL SEARCH AND STUDY

1. Often the New Testament uses the word *gift* in a general, universal sense, that is, of a gift received by all Christians. Examine each of the following references and identify the Churchwide gift that is mentioned: Acts 2:38; Romans 5:15–17; 2 Corinthians 9:8–15; and Romans 6:23.

2. In the New Testament, four significant references detail for the Church its spiritual gifts. These "gift lists" occur in Romans 12:3–8; 1 Corinthians 12:4–10, 27–28; Ephesians 4:1–13; and 1 Peter 4:7–11. What spiritual gifts are mentioned in these passages?

3. How many of these spiritual gifts are on your personal list?

4. Are you surprised that any of the gifts should be considered spiritual gifts? Do any of the gifts listed disturb you in any way? Do you think God still gives all these spiritual gifts to Christians today? Some people say that God gives some additional gifts to Christians today such as music, preaching, writing, and craftsmanship. Do you agree?

5. Why all these gifts? What does God have in mind? Read 1 Corinthians 12:7; 14:12; Ephesians 4:12–13; and 1 Peter 4:10. For what purposes does God give spiritual gifts to the Church?

WHAT THIS MEANS FOR US

1. Look at the list of spiritual gifts again. Which gift is most necessary in your congregation right now? (Choose two or three if you like.)

2. If Christian congregations were to take more seriously the matter of spiritual gifts and their use of them, what changes might be necessary in the structures and procedures of churches?

3. A Christian friend tells you that you haven't really been "filled with the Spirit" until you speak in tongues. He says this gift is the surest sign that one has been born again of the Spirit. Knowing what you know so far about spiritual gifts, how would you respond?

4. Look again at the section "Biblical Search and Study." Think about the "general gifts" (number 1) and the "spiritual gifts" (number 2) you have received. Do you feel more thankful for one type than for the other? Why or why not? How do you think God wants you to use your "general gifts"? your "spiritual gifts"?

GLEANINGS

Jot down a few insights into spiritual gifts that you learned from today's session.

SESSION 4

THE GIFTS (PART II)

THIS SESSION'S FOCUS

In session 3, you used four significant New Testament passages to build a list of spiritual gifts. Perhaps you can see why members of the Early New Testament Church felt so gifted. God's gifts were many and varied.

Though complete agreement is lacking, many students of the Bible group spiritual gifts this way:

Special people gifts—apostolicity; prophecy; evangelism; shepherding; teaching

Speaking gifts—exhortation; wisdom; knowledge

Serving gifts—serving; helping; leadership; administration; giving; showing mercy; discernment; faith; hospitality

Sign gifts—tongues; interpretation; healing; miracles

It's not always easy to designate a gift or grouping. For instance, in Ephesians 4, it's possible to designate one gift as pastor-teacher. The grammar in the passage (v. 11) allows for it. Yet in two other lists, the gift of teacher appears on its own. Students of Scripture must decide among several alternative listings: pastor, pastor-teacher, teacher, two of these, or all three.

In this session, we'll look more closely at each spiritual gift, find its occurrence in the Scriptures, and define it more sharply. All of this will move you closer to the point where you can more readily discover and use your own spiritual gift(s).

OBJECTIVES

By the power of the Holy Spirit working through God's Word, the participants will

- be familiar with special spiritual gifts in the Early New Testament Church;

- be able to define each special spiritual gift;

- broaden their understanding of the use of spiritual gifts in congregational life; and
- begin to identify their own special spiritual gifts.

MEDITATION

Today, Lord, Jim came and asked me to teach Sunday School again.

He's been after me for a year now.

What am I supposed to tell him?

Is it fair to say no again?

Or to put him off another year?

I heard once, Lord, of a Sunday School teacher who received an award for teaching fifty years.

Imagine it—fifty years!

Do You know what she said, Lord?

She said that fifty years ago, she had offered to teach as a substitute for one term!

Is Sunday School teaching a life sentence, Lord? Is it?

What does it take to be a good teacher?

Liking kids? Being patient? Preparation?

Or is Mr. Miller right when he says, "Good teachers carry big sticks from the start"?

Shall I try it, Lord?

Have you given me the gift of teaching?

Lord, before I talk to Jim, help me sort out my gifts.

But don't let me keep sorting and sorting and sorting.

Instead, fill me with conviction.

Then give me a sense of urgency.

Give me the courage to act.

Now. Amen.

Meet three members of Grace Church. They could belong to any church.

- Tom is the pastor of Grace Church. His people support and love him, but he lacks the confidence he once had. He questions his effectiveness, especially in his teaching and preaching. He still likes to call on members, visit the sick, and make evangelism visits. However, the preaching and the teaching have become a burden. Tom wonders if he should be in the ministry.

- Carol faces a potentially dangerous situation at work. For several months, she has known about a shady deal her boss made with one of the women on the staff. In return for sexual favors, he rewards the woman with extra benefits and assignments. It's getting harder for Carol to stay quiet. Her faith, she says, will not allow her to let the situation continue. She must confront both the boss and the co-worker. She knows her job will be on the line. Still, she has decided to speak up.

- Frank has always appreciated Dale's insight and wise counsel. They're good friends. Over coffee, Frank explains that he's leaving Grace Church. He tells Dale he thinks he'd be happier at a church that is more spiritually alive. But he wonders. Is this God's will or just his own need for change? Is God causing him to feel uncomfortable about leaving Grace, or is this a temptation on the part of the devil? Frank hopes Dale can help him understand.

1. Look again at the list of spiritual gifts. In each of these cases, what specific spiritual gifts are being used or being sought?

2. In your opinion, is it possible to be a pastor without having some of the gifts? If so, which ones are crucial? If not, why?

3. Why do you think some Christians are more willing to boldly confront difficult situations?

4. What would you tell Frank if he came to you for advice? He wants to be spiritually fulfilled. Is this an adequate reason for leaving his congregation?

BIBLICAL SEARCH AND STUDY

1. Take a closer look at spiritual gifts. As you do, carefully examine the following definitions and passages; explain how this gift works and what it accomplishes in the Church; suggest activities or ministries in the Church that would fully employ this gift.

a. *Apostolicity*—A particular Christian appointed by the Holy Spirit and empowered with special gifts for leading, inspiring, and developing the churches of God by the proclamation of the Gospel and the teaching of true doctrine (Acts 13–14). *Note:* Although qualities of the office of apostle and prophet exist today, most theologians teach that these offices do not exist today since none of us is an eyewitness to the resurrection (Acts 1:21–22). The once-for-all-times nature of these offices is stressed when St. Paul says the Church has been built (aorist passive tense of verb) on the foundation of the apostles and prophets (Ephesians 2:20).

b. *Prophecy*—A particular Christian appointed by the Holy Spirit and empowered with special gifts for communicating the Word of God to people (Acts 2:14–21; 11:27–30; 1 Corinthians 14:1–5, 30–33, 37–40).

c. *Evangelism*—A particular Christian appointed by the Holy Spirit and empowered with special gifts for presenting the Good News of Jesus Christ to non-Christians so that unbelievers become disciples of our Lord (Acts 21:8; 8:1–8, 26–40).

d. *Shepherding*—A particular Christian appointed by the Holy Spirit and empowered with special gifts for taking on the responsibility for the spiritual welfare of the community of God's people. (Pastor means "shepherd." "Pastor" and "elder" are used synonymously in the New Testament. See John 21:16; 1 Timothy 3:1–7; and Titus 1:5–9.)

e. *Teaching*—A particular Christian appointed by the Holy Spirit and empowered with special gifts for communicating the truths of God's Word so that others learn (Matthew 28:18–20; Acts 2:42; 13:1; James 3:1–5).

f. *Exhortation*—The special gift whereby the Holy Spirit enables particular Christians to stand alongside fellow Christians in need and bring them counsel and encouragement. (*Exhortation*, which means literally "to call to the side of," is sometimes translated "encouragement." See 1 Thessalonians 5:14; 2 Timothy 4:2; Titus 1:9; 2:15; and Hebrews 3:12–15.)

g. *Wisdom*—The special gift whereby the Holy Spirit enables particular Christians to bring to the Church an understanding of God's will for Christian living (1 Corinthians 1:18–25; 2 Timothy 3:15).

h. *Knowledge*—The special gift whereby the Holy Spirit enables particular Christians to understand the great truths of God's Word and to make them relevant to specific situations in the Church (Romans 11:33–36; 1 Corinthians 13:8–12).

i. *Serving*—The special gift whereby the Holy Spirit enables particular Christians to identify the needs of people (inside and outside the Church) and implement plans to meet those needs (John 13:1–17; Acts 6:1–3; 2 Corinthians 8:1–15).

j. *Helping*—The special gift whereby the Holy Spirit enables particular Christians to willingly bear the burdens of other Christians and so help others in the Church, thus enabling them to do their tasks more efficiently (Acts 20:34–35; Galatians 6:2; 2 Timothy 4:11).

k. *Leadership*—The special gift whereby the Holy Spirit enables particular Christians to motivate God's people, delegate responsibilities, and direct and inspire so that the Church's work goes on effectively (Exodus 18:13–26; 1 Thessalonians 5:12–13; 1 Timothy 5:17–22).

l. *Administration*—The special gift whereby the Holy Spirit enables particular Christians effectively to direct a segment of the Church's ministry, keeping the Church on course (Acts 14:23; 1 Timothy 5).

m. *Giving*—The special gift whereby the Holy Spirit enables particular Christians to offer their material blessings for the work of the Church with exceptional willingness, cheerfulness, and liberality (2 Corinthians 8:1–5; 9:6–15; Philippians 4:15–20).

n. *Showing mercy*—The special gift whereby the Holy Spirit provides particular Christians with an exceptional measure of love and compassion and moves them to devote large amounts of time and energy to care for the suffering. (See Romans 12:8 and Colossians 3:12. *Note:* The word in the original denotes strong emotional responses that come from the viscera, the "bowels" in Greek.)

o. *Discernment*—The special gift whereby the Holy Spirit enables particular Christians to distinguish with clarity between that which is of God and that which is of this world and of Satan (Acts 5:3–6; 8:18–23; 16:16–18; 1 John 4:1–6).

p. *Faith*—The special gift whereby the Holy Spirit provides particular Christians with unusual trust in God's promises, thus enabling them to take heroic stands for their Christian principles and to face danger, persecution, and pressure with confidence in God's power and presence (Hebrews 11; Acts 6:8–15).

q. *Hospitality*—The special gift whereby the Holy Spirit provides particular Christians with willing hearts, thus enabling them cheerfully to open their homes to others, offering them lodging, food, and fellowship (Luke 10:1–12; Acts 16:13–15; 1 Timothy 3:2; Hebrews 13:1–2; 1 Peter 4:9).

r. *Tongues*—The special gift whereby the Holy Spirit enables particular Christians to speak to God or to fellow Christians in a language they have never learned (1 Corinthians 14).

s. *Interpretation*—The special gift whereby the Holy Spirit enables particular Christians to translate that which is spoken in tongues for the Church (1 Corinthians 14:6–19, 26–33).

t. *Healing*—The special gift whereby the Holy Spirit uses particular Christians to restore health to the sick (Luke 9:1–2; Acts 3:1–16; 28:7–10; James 5:14–16).

u. *Miracles*—The special gift whereby the Holy Spirit uses particular Christians to perform mighty acts revealing God's power (John 14:12–14; Acts 6:8; 8:6–8).

2. Discuss the following questions,

a. Do any of the gifts appear to be similar? For example, what is the difference between the gift of leadership and the gift of administration? between wisdom and knowledge? between prophecy and exhortation?

b. Which gifts of the Spirit do you believe are present in your group right now?

c. Knowing what you do about the apostle Paul, which spiritual gifts would you say the Holy Spirit gave to him?

WHAT THIS MEANS FOR US

1. "Charismatic" churches usually place great emphasis on the sign gifts: tongues, interpretation, miracles, and healing. Are any of these gifts present in your congregation?

2. Paul emphasizes that people with spiritual gifts are gifts to the Church. How does this emphasis affect your attitude about all your spiritual gifts? How would you respond, for example, to someone in your congregation who announces that he has received the gift of healing?

3. Do you agree or disagree with this statement? "Not every Christian has the spiritual gift of an evangelist, but every Christian has the role of witnessing, or evangelism." (See 2 Timothy 4:5.) Give reasons for your answer.

4. Look at the list of spiritual gifts as you consider each of the following situations. What gift(s) is called for in each case?
a. An accident victim trying to decide why this has happened

b. A person making a financial pledge to the church

c. A church council planning meeting

d. A student disagreeing with a teacher on the basis of Scripture

e. A new congregation just getting started

f. An opportunity to begin a nursing home visitation ministry

g. A door-to-door canvass for Christ

h. A lunch for the surviving family after a funeral service

i. A terminally ill patient unwilling to accept death

5. In the next session, we'll work toward discovering our own spiritual gifts. Begin thinking about it now. What gift(s) do you seem to have? How are you using it (them) in the Church?

GLEANINGS

How many of the spiritual gifts can you list from memory? Put a check mark next to any that you feel you may have. Put an *X* next to those you wish to study in more detail.

SESSION 5

DISCOVERING YOUR SPIRITUAL GIFT(S)

THIS SESSION'S FOCUS

In the last session, you looked at Scripture passages and definitions of the various gifts of the Spirit. These gifts form a wonderful parade of attributes, actions, people, and skills that enable the Church to carry out its mission and ministry.

In this session, you'll do more than watch the parade go by. You'll start finding your place in the parade as you try to discover your own spiritual gift(s).

OBJECTIVES

By the power of the Holy Spirit working through God's Word, the participants will

- better understand how Christians can discover their spiritual gift(s);
- continue to discover or to reaffirm their spiritual gift(s); and
- recognize ways to use their gift(s) to build up the Church.

MEDITATION

Lord, the house down the street is a sight to behold!

It's green, blue, yellow, beige, and trimmed in brown.

The owner, it seems, has started painting his home several times, changing the color scheme along the way, but never finishing the job.

The children call it "the house of many colors."

For me, the house is a stark parable of having many good starts and few finishes—of not following through.

Sometimes, Lord, I've felt that way about my work in the Church.

I've tried many things, held many offices.

At times, I've worn more hats than I could manage.

Too many times, I started something but didn't finish well.

Lord, help me find my niche in the church.

Teach me to seek and to use my gifts to the fullest, so that my life in the church does not look like a house of many colors.

Teach me, Lord, to start with the best I have from Your Spirit and to focus on doing well what I can do best. Amen.

SESSION PRIMER

Evaluate each of the following situations, using these questions: Do you think the situation shows good judgment? Can you see yourself or your congregation doing the same thing? What might prevent similar circumstances from happening?

1. For years, Grace Church held elections of church officers in which people ran against each other, some losing, some winning. Now Grace has changed its constitution and bylaws; now no one loses an election. Instead, the members of Grace Church have identified their spiritual gifts and are chosen by a selection committee to serve in areas of ministry for which they are especially gifted. Every year, the congregation "elects" no fewer than 190 people for specific ministries in the congregation. Now everyone wins; the whole slate of candidates is elected without people running against each other. Gifts are simply matched to ministries.

2. People are surprised, but Jill has been adamant in her decision. For years, she was busy in many church activities, often harried and frustrated. This year, she has decided to focus on the one ministry that has always brought her the most joy: teaching Sunday School. When asked to serve on other committees or to head up other projects, she responds, "No, thank you. I'm a teacher, and I want to teach well." She feels her teaching has improved greatly, and she has never felt more fulfilled in her church work.

3. Everyone agrees: Jim would make a great pastor. Jim has the dream himself; however, he and his family do not have the financial resources to put him through the seminary. Jim and his wife, Linda, have five children, including two toddlers. Recently, the congregation did an amazing thing. Recognizing Jim's gift, they decided to pay the full tuition for his seminary training. He will begin his studies next fall.

BIBLICAL SEARCH AND STUDY

Talk through the following questions in your whole group.

1. Read 1 Corinthians 1:4–7. Paul is writing to a gifted congregation. Later, in chapters 12–14, he exhorts them to recognize their spiritual gifts, to appreciate them as gifts from God, and to use them in the proper way. Now read 12:31a and 14:1. The process of recognizing one's spiritual gift(s) involves earnestly seeking those gifts from God. What motivates Christians to seek or earnestly desire spiritual gifts? For what wrong reason might Christians seek spiritual gifts? According to 14:12, what should be the central motivation for gift seeking?

2. Christians who desire spiritual gifts often pray that God will enable them to discover their gifts. Describe the prayer and the outcome of prayer in each of the following passages: Luke 11:9–13; Colossians 1:9–10; and 1 Corinthians 14:13. You may wish to discuss the role of prayer in the ministry of your congregation. Are you a praying church? Is your church's ministry characterized by specific prayers to recognize, appreciate, and properly use the gifts of God?

3. Now read Romans 12:6a. Recognizing the variety of gifts in the Church, Paul says, "Let us use them." How should they be used

according to 1 Corinthians 12:7 and 14:12? If we do nothing, we certainly do not build up the Church, nor do we grow in our ability to use our spiritual gifts. Paul takes this even further. His beautiful celebration of Christian love in 1 Corinthians 13 is understood best in its context—a discussion of spiritual gifts. Read the chapter, beginning with 12:31 and reading through 14:1. In what sense is Christian love the ideal setting for discovering and using spiritual gifts?

What This Means for Us

A Tool for Discovering One's Spiritual Gifts

Answer the following questions. They are designed to help you identify your spiritual gifts—or at least to begin the process.

1. *Life purposes.* Spiritual gifts are a part of one's whole life picture. We all have some central values and purposes that shape our actions and attitudes. We're most fulfilled when we are true to our life purposes—our vocations or callings.

In the space that follows, list three such callings, or central life purposes, that characterize your life right now. Examples of these are a desire to make people happy, a yearning to relieve suffering, a need to be creative and innovative, and a wish to spread beauty or to bring organization and structure to life. Think about your life, your personality, your history, and your dreams. Then list three purposes.

Now look at the list of spiritual gifts in session 4 of this study guide. Which gifts appear best to fulfill your life purposes? List all that seem relevant.

2. *My ministries.* You've probably been involved in some of your church's ministries—maybe many, maybe just a few. List as many of these experiences as you can, especially those from recent years. When your list is complete, circle those that brought you the greatest satisfaction and fulfillment. (You may circle many or just one or two.) Then check those items that brought frustrations and burdens instead of satisfaction.

Now look at the ministries you circled. Try to match these ministries with the spiritual gifts from session 4. Jot down the spiritual gifts expressed in your fulfilling ministries.

3. *Affirmation.* Affirmation from other members of the Body of Christ can help you discover your spiritual gifts. Very often, this affirmation assures us that we've found our niche in the Church's ministry. (Remember, though, that God does not promise that affirmation will always come our way as we practice our spiritual gifts. A cross may come instead.)

Think about a time when you were affirmed by a fellow Christian or spiritual leader in your congregation. What gift had you practiced? Refer again to the list of gifts. You may be able to think of more than one experience of affirmation. Jot down the spiritual gifts practiced and affirmed in each instance.

4. *Changes.* Perhaps you sense a need for some changes concerning your work in the Church. What should change? Specifically, on what ministries would you like to focus most? What gift or gifts do these ministries express?

5. *Discoveries.* Look at your responses to items 1–4. What spiritual gift(s) surfaced frequently? That is, what spiritual gift(s) appear to relate best to your calling, your fulfilling ministries, the affirmation of Christ's people, and your own need for change or focus?

To FOLLOW UP

1. Briefly share your responses.
2. Did the tool help you discover anything about yourself or about your spiritual gift(s)? Explain.
3. Suggest opportunities to use the gift(s) you identified within your congregation.
4. Provide ways to use the gift(s) to build up the Church in your community.

GLEANINGS

If you are not sure you have recognized your spiritual gift(s), continue to "earnestly desire" it through prayer. If you feel you have discovered one or more gifts, ask God to bless and direct your efforts to use each gift for the common good.

SESSION 6

THE MORE EXCELLENT WAY

THIS SESSION'S FOCUS

Some gifted people never learn to use their gifts in the right way. A gifted artist may focus so much on his own genius that his self-consciousness and conceit stifle his creativity. A fine athlete may become less effective by being nasty and unkind to her opponents or even to her own teammates. A skilled surgeon's ambition and the taste of fame may so blind him that he begins to lose his dedication to patients.

Similar abuse can occur with our use of spiritual gifts in the Church. Congregations blessed with spiritual gifts sometimes drag people along sleepily, neglecting their ministries, or they become embroiled in destructive conflicts. People may show little concern for harmony or peace as they practice their gifts; they may struggle for supremacy or become judgmental with one another.

The Church suffers through all of this, and the Spirit's gifts receive a tarnished image among God's people. Through all these human weaknesses, God continues to pour out His grace to His people. The Spirit provides His Church with gifts and also blesses us with the character we need to use His gifts well. The fruit of the Spirit make up this character. The same Spirit who gives gifts to His Church also provides the fruit. These fruit enable us to use the gifts for the common good.

How are fruit of the Spirit different from spiritual gifts? You recall that God gives spiritual gifts (as we use the term in this course) to whom He wills, when and how He wills. Spiritual gifts are given selectively, and we each have only one or a few gifts. Fruit, on the other hand, are "all for all." God gives all the fruit of the Spirit for all Christians. We can all desire them, pray for them, work for them, and grow in them. The fruit of the Spirit, which are given by the Holy Spirit, grow in our Christian lives as we grow in the Lord through His Word and Sacraments.

OBJECTIVES

By the power of the Holy Spirit working through God's Word, the participants will

- become more aware of the need for love to be central in their use of the Spirit's gifts;
- recognize the fruit of the Spirit as traits complementing every use of spiritual gifts in the Church; and
- seek the unity of their congregation through the gifts and fruit of the Spirit.

MEDITATION

Lord, it's good to be where love abounds.

Maybe that's one reason why I'm so grateful for our church.

Love thrives among us, Lord—a good and true fruit of the Holy Spirit

I see it in the eyes of our people, this love.

I see it in how we huddle together after church, as if our church is somehow bigger and richer than just the morning service.

Some people especially seem to nurture that love.

You know who they are, Lord. They work peace among us.

They are the smile on the face of the Body of Christ in the place we call our church home.

Lord, You know how grateful I am for the gifts You've given our congregation.

We are not a poor church, Lord.

We are rich in gifts and in ministries!

Today, though, I sing Your praises for our church's character, a blessing from Your Spirit as well.

Gifts are best given and received in an atmosphere of love and joy and peace.

So thank You, Lord, for the Spirit in our church. Amen.

Session Primer

Read aloud the following news article. Then use the questions that follow to discuss the article.

Peace Church, Valley City, Closes Doors

(Valley City) Peace Church, Valley City, closed its doors yesterday after a final service attended by thirty-two. Founded in 1922, the church once claimed a membership of eight hundred souls.

In recent years, the church has been involved in a series of conflicts, including legal battles in the courts. Ten years ago, the church's most recent pastor, William Lauder, arrived and began an active community outreach program. The church added day care, food and clothing closets, and lodging for the homeless to its programs.

For a while, Peace Church grew. Neighborhood people became church members. The leadership of the church also changed. In the process, many of the church's former leaders felt disenfranchised and disagreed with Lauder's community emphasis. A large group left the church to join nearby Trinity.

A second struggle occurred when a group of about a hundred members of Peace formed a charismatic prayer and praise group and met regularly at the church for their own services of prayer, tongues, and healing. The group pressured the pastor to renew the church with charismatic fervor, but met with little success. Lauder took a call elsewhere, and the group left to form their own church, Holy Spirit Church, a mile from Peace.

Since then, Peace has been embroiled in controversies over the sale of the land, the calling of a minister, the authority of elders in the church during a pastoral vacancy, and the church's support of various community organizations.

Many who joined the church during Pastor's Lauder's ministry left soon after his departure. Most of the community outreach programs have been discontinued. The church has been without a pastor for three years. An attempt to sell some of the church's property to pay outstanding debts has led to a struggle in the courts among church leaders.

When asked to describe what has happened to his former church, Pastor Lauder responded, "We grew everything at Peace except the fruit of the Spirit. We're all to blame, myself included. If we could do it all again, we'd do it differently, I know."

1. What factors, in your opinion, most directly led to the demise of Peace Church?

2. What might have been done differently at Peace?

3. What does the story show about the use of the gifts of the Spirit in the congregation?

BIBLICAL SEARCH AND STUDY

Discuss the following questions.

1. Read 1 Corinthians 12:31–13:13. Why do you think Paul so emphasized the need for love in the Church? What may have been happening in the Church at Corinth to prompt Paul's chapter on love? (For clues, see 1 Corinthians 12:20–21; 14:4, 26–33a.)

2. Read Galatians 5:16–26. Verses 22–23 list the fruit of the Spirit. These fruit may be defined as follows:

Love—The Christian character trait whereby God empowers us to seek the highest good of another, no matter the cost or sacrifice involved, and no matter how "deserving" the other may or may not be.

Joy—The Christian character trait whereby God enables us to find delight in the Lord, regardless of the circumstances of our lives.

Peace—The Christian character trait whereby God enables us to find wholeness and quietness of heart in the conviction that we are the Lord's.

Patience—The Christian character trait whereby God empowers us to be forbearing and forgiving with others, as our Lord is with us.

Kindness—The Christian character trait whereby God empowers us to be considerate and benevolent toward others, not irking or provoking them.

Goodness—The Christian character trait whereby God empowers us to express our sincere goodwill toward others at every point, even if it means criticism and rebuke.

Faithfulness—The Christian character trait whereby God empowers us to be trustworthy and reliable in our relationships with others.

Gentleness—The Christian character trait whereby God enables us to be submissive to His will, open to being taught, and compassionate for others' needs and emotions.

Self-control—The Christian character trait whereby God causes us to discipline ourselves so that we can serve others.

Now go back and circle the fruit you wish to nurture and need most right now as you consider your use of your spiritual gifts in the Church. Second, underline the fruit most needed by your congregation at this time. Third, place a check mark next to the fruit of the Spirit that are growing well in your congregation's spiritual garden.

Finally, share and explain your responses.

3. Look at the list of fruit of the Spirit again. List an antonym (opposite) for each fruit. Why would these character traits cause division and conflict in the church?

4. Discuss ways the nine spiritual fruit can be nurtured. What are the means God has given His Church to enhance and strengthen our attitudes and character?

5. Think of a time when God enabled you to display one or more of the fruit of the Spirit in your personal life. Then think of a time when you displayed the antonym instead. If you feel comfortable doing so, share some of your feelings about these times.

Think again about ways to nurture the fruit. What commitments to nurture are you willing to make? How can the members of your class support one another in nurture?

What This Means for Us

1. Spiritual gifts are evident in the Church through ministries and activities that Christians undertake. Fruit of the Spirit are the attitudes and character with which Christians use their gifts. In this context, the Spirit's gifts can be a real blessing in the Church.

Divide your class into two groups. Together you represent a Christian congregation at work in ministry. Group A should represent the worldly traits that sometimes mark the church. You may wish to refer to the antonyms you listed under question 3 above. Group B should represent the fruit of the Spirit at work in the church. They will express the Christian traits that move the congregation ahead in ministry.

Role-play the following situations according to your group assignment. Members of Group A may speak to the situation on the basis of, for example, party spirit, impatience, or anger. Members of Group B may respond on the basis of, for example, kindness, gentleness, or self-control.

a. It has been moved and seconded that every member of your congregation be involved in an all-area evangelism canvass.

b. People are complaining that your new pastor is changing too much too fast.

c. A council member recommends that you fund the education of a congregation member who will train at a synodical school to be a Christian teacher.

d. A member of your church began to speak in tongues at a Bible class last Sunday morning.

e. Your pastor and the principal of your Christian Day School do not get along and often clash at meetings.

f. Your congregation is seriously divided over a proposal to build a new sanctuary.

g. Your congregation's young people are asking for financial support for a service project at a nearby nursing home.

What did you learn from your role-played conversations? Think back to what was said. How many worldly and spiritual traits can you list that were reflected in the conversations? Did any of the situations hit close to home? In each of the situations discussed, what spiritual gifts were at stake?

2. Choose one of the fruit of the Spirit that you feel you need and wish to nurture most right now. How would your life change if you lived according to that fruit? What would be different about you or about your

role in the church? Share your responses with your group. Then pray for one another that the Spirit will grant this fruit.

GLEANINGS

On a separate sheet of paper, review your discoveries during this course. Jot down your surprises, your learnings, and your resolutions for the future. "Having gifts that differ according to the grace given to us, let us use them" (Romans 12:6).

APPENDIX

The following quotations are taken from *The Lutheran Church and the Charismatic Movement,* a report by the Commission on Theology and Church Relations (CTCR) of The Lutheran Church—Missouri Synod, April 1977.

> The church will accept with joy and gratitude any gift which the Spirit in His grace may choose to bestow on us for the purpose of edifying the body of Christ. It will recognize that the Lord does not forsake His church but promises the abiding presence of His Spirit. The church, therefore, will not reject out of hand the possibility that God may in His grace and wisdom endow some in Christendom with the same abilities and powers He gave His church in past centuries. It will take care lest it quench the Spirit by failing to expect or pray for God's presence and power in building His church. But it will also take seriously the admonition of the apostle to "test the spirits to see whether they are of God; for many false prophets have gone out into the world" (1 John 4:1 [RSV]; cf. also 1 Cor. 12:10). Above all, the church will not employ such gifts as though they were means of grace [pp. 5–6].

> *The gift of the Holy Spirit does not necessarily include extraordinary spiritual gifts.* While Lutherans rejoice in the gracious promise that the gift of the Holy Spirit will be given to all generations of believers (Acts 2:39), neither the Scriptures nor the Lutheran Confessions support the view that this gift of the Spirit necessarily includes such extraordinary spiritual gifts as tongues, miracles, miraculous healings, and prophecy (1 Cor. 12). According to the pattern revealed in the Bible, God does not necessarily give His church in all ages the same special gifts. He bestows His blessings according to His good pleasure (1 Cor. 12:11) [p. 9].

LEADER GUIDE

SOME PRACTICAL TIPS

We gathered together experienced Bible class teachers—pastors, district presidents, and lay leaders—and we asked them, "What tips would you pass on to a discussion leader for a course such as this?"

Their advice is this:

- Arrive early enough to set up the room. Make sure that the seating is arranged so that everyone can see and be seen.
- If the setting permits it, serve refreshments, such as coffee, tea, soft drinks, fruit, cookies, or cake.
- Bring extra Bibles in case some people forget to bring their own. Supply hymnals too.
- Encourage participants to be specific in their responses.
- Avoid succumbing to the temptation to say, "Let's see what the 'answer book' (this Leader Guide) says."
- Encourage everyone to participate, without putting anyone on the spot.
- Limit your remarks to the necessary information so you don't monopolize the discussion. Listen! And be like John the Baptizer: decrease, so that Christ and these people may increase.
- Encourage others to share their thoughts and feelings.
- Be well prepared for each session through prior study and prayer. By all means, read through the Study Guide, the Leader Guide, and the Scripture references beforehand, taking notes.
- Help others share by reflecting or "playing back" their comments. Repeating questions or comments spoken by others will also help those with hearing impairments. Repeat them in a different way in order to encourage more depth and sharing.
- Find ways to keep one or two people from monopolizing the conversation. Similarly, do not allow these sessions to become excuses to complain about the pastor, church, or other people. After all, this is a Bible study, not a gripe session.

- Since you are the leader, you also serve as timekeeper. Begin and end on time. If you meet on Sunday morning—before, after, or between worship services—you probably need to keep the sessions to between 45 minutes and an hour. If you meet during the week, you might extend the time to an hour and a half.

- Be selective with this material! As the writers and editors of these courses, we'd rather give you too much than too little. There's no need to use all of it. While preparing, check or circle the material you want to use and cross out the material you will not use. We may write the script, but you are the director, and your participants are the actors. You know far better than we do what is needed in your congregation.

- Finally, ask the Holy Spirit to guide you through this course.

God's blessings to you as you lead this study!

SESSION 1

THE GIFTED

THIS SESSION'S FOCUS

Read aloud and then discuss briefly the session focus.

OBJECTIVES

Invite participants to silently read the objectives.

MEDITATION

Invite a volunteer to read the meditation aloud. Then provide time for silent prayer.

SESSION PRIMER

Ask, **What are spiritual gifts?** Write participants' responses on the chalkboard or dry-erase board. Accept all responses. Then say, **In this study we will use the following definition of spiritual gifts.** Direct participants' attention to the definition in the study guide. Read aloud the definition. Ask, **What do you think about this definition?** Provide participants an opportunity to tell whether they agree or disagree with the three statements and why. Tell participants that they will find the answers to these questions and others as they search God's Word for information about spiritual gifts.

BIBLICAL SEARCH AND STUDY

Tell participants that they will search the Scriptures to discover the giftedness of Christ's Church. You may study as a whole class, or if your class is large, you may wish to divide it into smaller groups. Assign a different set of questions to each group. If you divide the class into small groups, make sure you give each group a chance to report their findings to the entire class.

1. Christians owe their giftedness to God's grace. Jesus became poor, humbling Himself to live, suffer, and die on the cross, so that we might become rich. Our richness is the forgiveness of sins and eternal life Jesus won for us on the cross.

2. Paul gives thanks to God for His grace given to the Corinthian Christians in Christ Jesus. Through His grace, the Corinthians were enriched in every way and did not lack any spiritual gift.

Explain that *grace* (*charis* in Greek) and *gift* (*charisma* in Greek; plural: *charismata*) are often tied together in the New Testament. When early Christians considered their gifts, they saw God's grace as the source of those gifts. Interestingly, *joy* (*chara* in Greek) and *thanksgiving* (*eucharistia*) belong to the same family of *char* words—a happy family, indeed!

Read Romans 12:6a; Ephesians 4:7–8; and 1 Peter 4:10. We each have different gifts, given to us according to God's grace. We serve Him and His Church as we use whatever gifts He has given us to share His grace with others.

3. A lack of repentance and a lack of love will cause a gifted congregation to grow stale and cold. As members of one Body, Christians are called to peace. Demonstrating joy and giving thanks always is God's will for us in Christ Jesus. Give thanks to God, for everything He created is good.

4. Although answers will vary, some truisms might include (a) the body includes many parts; (b) all parts of the body have varying but necessary functions; and (c) the parts of the body work together for the good of the whole body.

5. Christians, through their words and actions, are living stones built into a spiritual house that serves God. We are a priesthood of believers, a people belonging to God. God asks every Christian to offer himself or herself as a living sacrifice, holy and pleasing to God.

WHAT THIS MEANS FOR US

Invite a volunteer to read aloud the letter to the pastor. Then discuss the questions that follow.

1. Linda is bummed out. She has served her congregation in many ways. Instead of identifying her gifts and focusing her service to best use

her gifts, Linda has volunteered to do everything. Linda needs to hear of God's intense love for her in Jesus Christ. Linda needs rest and an opportunity to regroup.

2. Remind participants that mandates that begin with "you should" or "you ought" are statements of Law. The Law will not effectively motivate people to use their gifts, to give thanks, or to demonstrate joy. Only the Gospel, the Good News of God's love for us in Jesus Christ, calls us to repentance and motivates us to use our gifts in service to Him, to give thanks, and to demonstrate joy. In other words, God's grace alone will empower and enable people to serve God through their words and actions.

3. Answers will vary. Ask participants to suggest ways to remedy the situation described by the pastor. Remind participants that the Holy Spirit works through God's Word and Sacraments to strengthen faith, motivating and equipping God's people for service.

4. Answers will vary.

GLEANINGS

Answers will vary. Allow participants to share what they have learned in this lesson about God's gifted people and His gifts to His people.

SESSION 2

THE GIVER

THIS SESSION'S FOCUS

Ask, **What do you know about the Holy Spirit and His work?** Write participants' responses on the chalkboard or dry-erase board. Accept all responses. Keep participants' responses in a visible place in the classroom throughout this session.

Invite a volunteer to read aloud the introductory paragraphs.

OBJECTIVES

Have participants silently read the objectives.

MEDITATION

Provide the class time for silent prayer after a volunteer reads aloud the meditation in the study guide.

SESSION PRIMER

Read aloud the quotation. Then discuss the questions that follow. The Holy Spirit comes where and when it pleases God to send Him.

BIBLICAL SEARCH AND STUDY

1. You may wish to divide the class into small groups and assign several passages to each group. Remind participants to summarize what each reference says about the Holy Spirit, focusing specifically on the nature and work of the Holy Spirit. Refer to the descriptions you wrote at the beginning of the class session. Modify the list as appropriate, recording key verbs and descriptive words to provide a summary of your group's search and study.

2. a. The Holy Spirit has all who believe in Jesus as their Lord and Savior.

b. The Holy Spirit, through the Word and Sacraments, freely gives to all Christians the most precious gifts: faith in Christ, the forgiveness of sins, and eternal life. In apostolic times, the Holy Spirit also gave some Christians the gift to perform miraculous signs and wonders (e.g., healings, speaking in tongues, raising the dead). The Scriptures do not teach that God will necessarily give all Christians in every time and place special miraculous gifts. The Holy Spirit gives according to His good pleasure. The Spirit's gifts are meant to build up the Body of Christ.

c. It is only by the power of the Holy Spirit working through God's Word and Sacraments that people believe and confess that Jesus Christ is Lord. Also, the fruit of the Spirit is evidence of the Holy Spirit's presence (Galatians 5:22–23) in His people and in His Church.

d. All the gifts of the Holy Spirit are given to be used in the Church and to build up the Church. The Holy Spirit gives people different gifts to be used in and by the Church.

3. Answers will vary. The Holy Spirit works through God's Word and Sacraments. When the study and proclamation of God's Word is neglected, the people lack the confidence and power necessary to build up the Church. However, despite our failings, the power of the Spirit to guide the Church is as great now as ever.

4. The Holy Spirit works through God's Word and Sacraments. A person seeking the Giver and His gifts can attend worship regularly, rely on God's promises given us in Baptism, receive the Lord's Supper often, study God's Word privately, and attend group Bible studies.

WHAT THIS MEANS FOR US

Have participants complete the questions individually or in small groups. Allow time for volunteers to share their responses.

1. Answers will vary. Again, help participants recognize that any program for spiritual renewal must begin and end with use of the Means of Grace—God's Word and Sacraments.

2–3. Accept all responses.

GLEANINGS

Take a few moments to allow volunteers to share what they have learned in this session.

SESSION 3

THE GIFTS (PART I)

THIS SESSION'S FOCUS

Read aloud this section. Review the definition of *spiritual gifts* provided in session 1. Discuss what spiritual gifts *are not*. Say, **In this session, we will build a spiritual gift list on the basis of Scripture.**

OBJECTIVES

Invite participants to silently read the objectives, or ask a volunteer to read them aloud.

MEDITATION

Allow time for silent prayer after a volunteer reads the meditation aloud to the class.

SESSION PRIMER

Ask for a volunteer to read the part of speaker 1 and another to read speaker 2. Then discuss the questions that follow with the entire class or, if your class is large, in small groups.

1. Although answers will vary, many people probably are unaware of, fail to seek, or do not desire the gifts.

2. Some congregations are so caught up in business that they may fail to identify the gifts of their people and to recognize how those gifts might be used to build up the Church. Others find the topic tricky to discuss and difficult to understand, something that this study seeks to address.

3. There may be missed opportunities for the Church to grow when people fail to "open" their gifts.

BIBLICAL SEARCH AND STUDY

1. The Holy Spirit provides the following Churchwide gifts: forgiveness of sins and the Spirit Himself (Acts 2:38); grace and righteousness that bring justification (Romans 5:15–17; 2 Corinthians 9:8–15); and eternal life (Romans 6:23).

2. Refer back to the definition of spiritual gifts in "This Session's Focus" in the study guide. Note that spiritual gifts, as we will consider them, are distinct and special gifts, different from the general gifts held in common by all Christians. All God's gifts, however, are worthy of discovery and celebration. Divide the class into four groups. Assign one of the four lists to each group. Each group should carefully search its assigned references and record a list of the spiritual gifts mentioned in the passage. When all the groups have completed their gift lists, ask for a report from each group.

Romans 12:3–8 lists prophesying, serving, teaching, encouraging (exhorting), generosity, leadership, and showing mercy.

1 Corinthians 12:4–10, 27–28 lists the message of wisdom, the message of knowledge, faith, healing, miraculous powers, prophecy, distinguishing between spirits, speaking in different tongues, and the interpretation of tongues.

Ephesians 4:1–13 teaches that some people are given to be apostles, prophets, evangelists, pastors, and teachers—all callings of the pastoral office.

1 Peter 4:7–11 lists hospitality, speaking, and serving.

3–4. Answers will vary. Remind participants that the Holy Spirit gifts His Church in order to build up the Church. Read aloud the following quote from *The Lutheran Church and the Charismatic Movement*, a 1977 document from the Commission on Theology and Church Relations (CTCR) of The Lutheran Church—Missouri Synod found in the Appendix on page 45.

5. Spiritual gifts are given by God for the common good of the Church (1 Corinthians 12:7), to build up the Church (1 Corinthians 14:12), to prepare God's people for works of ministry (Ephesians 4:12–13), and to serve others (1 Peter 4:10).

What This Means for Us

1. Answers will vary.

2. Answers will vary. Remind participants that the Holy Spirit gifts His people as their faith is strengthened through the Means of Grace.

3. Refer to the quotation from *The Lutheran Church and the Charismatic Movement*. Remind participants that it is contrary to the Holy Scriptures—and therefore dangerous to the salvation of people—to teach "that a Christian who has not had such an experience has an incomplete faith, is unconverted," or that sanctification is incomplete (CTCR, 1977, p. 11).

4. God desires that we use all of His gifts to build up His Church.

Gleanings

Have participants complete the activity individually and share their responses with a partner or in a small group.

SESSION 4

THE GIFTS (PART II)

THIS SESSION'S FOCUS

Read aloud or have volunteers read aloud this section. The gifts discussed in session 3 are categorized as *special people gifts, speaking gifts, serving gifts,* and *sign gifts.*

OBJECTIVES

Have participants read silently the objectives for this session.

MEDITATION

Ask someone to read the meditation aloud. Then take a few moments for silent prayer.

SESSION PRIMER

Read aloud each of the three vignettes about members of Grace Church.

1. Have participants match gifts with what we are told about each person. Answers will vary.

- Tom seems to possess the gifts of serving, helping, and/or giving. Point out that God has gifted pastors in different ways. Not all will possess the same gifts.

- Carol may possess or seek the gifts of exhortation and/or discernment in dealing with the problem she has encountered.

- Dale may possess or seek the gifts of wisdom and/or knowledge to help him provide answers to Frank.

2. God bestows on pastors His blessings according to His good pleasure. Not all pastors will possess the same gifts. God calls pastors into ministry to build up His Church with the gifts He has given them.

3. Faith strengthened by the power of the Holy Spirit working through God's Word and Sacraments enables Christians to boldly confront difficult situations.

4. Answers will vary. Remind participants that sometimes God places us in congregations that may seem lacking so that He may use our gifts to strengthen the congregation. It may be a time to serve rather than just be served.

BIBLICAL SEARCH AND STUDY

1. Read and discuss the list of gifts provided in the study guide. Read one or more of the passages listed after each gift to provide participants with a clearer understanding of the role and use of these gifts.

2. a. Some gifts may seem similar, but most will have differences from the others.

b. Answers will vary. This question provides group members an opportunity to affirm one another's giftedness.

c. St. Paul had the gifts of shepherding and evangelism. Participants may suggest additional gifts that St. Paul exhibited.

WHAT THIS MEANS FOR US

1. Review the following quote from the CTCR document *The Lutheran Church and the Charismatic Movement* (p. 9) found in the Appendix on page 45.

2. Spiritual gifts must benefit the Church and help to build up the Church. We need to take seriously the admonition of the apostle to "test the spirits to see whether they are from God, for many false prophets have gone out into the world" (1 John 4:1).

3. Agree. Not every Christian has the spiritual gift of an evangelist, but Jesus commands all of His followers, "You will be My witnesses" (Acts 1:8).

4. Answers will vary. Accept all reasonable responses.

5. This question gives participants the opportunity to begin thinking about the gifts they have received from the Holy Spirit.

GLEANINGS

Suggest that participants complete this activity before the next session.

DISCOVERING YOUR SPIRITUAL GIFT(S)

THIS SESSION'S FOCUS

Read aloud or invite a volunteer to read aloud the opening paragraphs.

OBJECTIVES

Ask participants to silently read the objectives.

MEDITATION

Ask someone to read the meditation aloud. Then take a few moments for participants to offer individual prayers.

SESSION PRIMER

Have participants work in small groups to evaluate the situations using the questions in the study guide.

BIBLICAL SEARCH AND STUDY

1. Faith strengthened as the Holy Spirit works through Word and Sacrament motivates a person to seek spiritual gifts from God. Christians desire to serve God using the gifts the Holy Spirit has provided them. A Christian should not seek spiritual gifts for personal gain or fortune. The central motivation for seeking gifts is to build up the Church.

2. Luke 11:9–13 emphasizes that the Father invites us to ask in order to receive and that the Father will give the Holy Spirit to those who ask Him! Colossians 1:9–10 emphasizes that we should pray without ceasing that all people would receive the knowledge of God's will through spiritual wisdom and understanding. The emphasis in 1 Corinthians 14:13 is that anyone who speaks in a tongue should pray for interpretation of the tongue, praying for guidance in the effective use of a spiritual gift.

3. Spiritual gifts should be used to build up the Church. In a setting where people demonstrate Christian love, we have the freedom to use the gifts God has given to us and to affirm others in their use of God's gifts.

WHAT THIS MEANS FOR US

A TOOL FOR DISCOVERING ONE'S SPIRITUAL GIFTS

Urge all participants to answer the questions in the study guide. These questions will help them identify the gifts the Holy Spirit has provided to them. Remind participants that their life purposes may not be the same as God's purposes for their lives. We must always pray for God's guidance so that in all situations, we may serve Him.

Allow participants the opportunity to share their discoveries with a partner or in small groups. Urge participants to use the follow-up suggestions to guide their sharing.

GLEANINGS

Urge participants to complete the suggested activity during the days and weeks ahead as they seek to discover and use their spiritual gifts.

SESSION 6

THE MORE EXCELLENT WAY

THIS SESSION'S FOCUS

Read aloud or invite volunteers to read aloud the opening paragraphs.

OBJECTIVES

Ask participants to silently read the objectives.

MEDITATION

Provide time for silent prayers after a volunteer reads aloud the meditation.

SESSION PRIMER

Invite a volunteer to read aloud the news story. Then use the follow-up questions to discuss the article.

1. Although answers will vary, internal strife, unwillingness to reach out into the community, and lack of leadership led to the demise of the church.

2. Training and equipping lay leadership would have enabled the congregation to remain strong, even when the pastor left the congregation. By having more of an emphasis on studying God's Word and growing a spirit of love within the congregation, it would have been easier for them to work with a spirit of cooperation and a focus on sharing the Gospel.

3. By setting personal agendas as a priority, the people neglected and obscured their spiritual gifts and the will of God to share the Gospel—His love in Christ. The fruit of the Spirit grow as God's people are strengthened by the power of the Holy Spirit working through God's Word and His Sacraments.

Biblical Search and Study

1. Love motivates Christians to serve others with their gifts and to affirm the gifts of other Christians. Without love, people can become jealous, cynical, angry, and so on toward one another.

2. Read aloud and discuss the various fruit of the Spirit. After reading the list, have participants circle up to three fruit they most desire as they consider the use of their spiritual gifts in the Church. Then have participants underline no more than three fruit most needed by their congregation. Finally, have participants place a check mark next to the fruit of the Spirit that are growing well in their congregation. Answers will vary.

3. Answers will vary.

4. God nurtures (grows) fruit as the Holy Spirit works through God's Word and Sacraments.

5. Allow participants to share as they feel comfortable doing so. Urge them to develop a plan whereby they have greater opportunity to experience the power of the Holy Spirit working through God's Word.

What This Means for Us

1. Select at least one or two vignettes for participants to role-play.

2. Agree to continue praying for one another during the days, weeks, and months ahead.

Gleanings

Have participants work independently to write things they discovered during this course. Then provide time for participants to share their discoveries with the entire class.